Read & Respond

FOR KS2

Read & Respond

FOR
KS2

Authors: Gill Friel and James Friel

Commissioning Editor: Rachel Mackinnon

Development Editor: Gemma Cary

Editor: Alex Albrighton

Assistant Editor: Vicky Butt

Series Designer: Anna Oliwa

Designer: Liz Gilbert

Cover Image: Quentin Blake

Illustrations: Quentin Blake and Mike Phillips/Beehive Illustration

Text © 2010 Gill Friel and James Friel © 2010 Scholastic Ltd

Designed using Adobe InDesign

Published by Scholastic Ltd,
Book End, Range Road, Witney,
Oxfordshire OX29 0YD
www.scholastic.co.uk

Printed by Bell & Bain
1 2 3 4 5 6 7 8 9   0 1 2 3 4 5 6 7 8 9

British Library Cataloguing-in-Publication Data
A catalogue record for this book is available
from the British Library.
ISBN 978-1407-11849-9

The rights of Gill Friel and James Friel to be identified as the authors of this work have been asserted by them in accordance with the Copyright, Designs and Patents Act 1988.

Extracts from the Primary National Strategy's *Primary Framework for Literacy* (2006) nationalstrategies.standards.dcsf.gov.uk/primary/primaryframework/literacyframework © Crown copyright. Reproduced under the terms of the Click Use Licence.

All rights reserved. This book is sold subject to the condition that it shall not, by way of trade or otherwise, be lent, hired out or otherwise circulated without the publisher's prior consent in any form of binding or cover other than that in which it is published and without a similar condition, including this condition, being imposed upon the subsequent purchaser.

No part of this publication may be reproduced, stored in a retrieval system, or transmitted, in any form or by any means, electronic, mechanical, photocopying, recording or otherwise, without the prior permission of the publisher. This book remains copyright, although permission is granted to copy pages where indicated for classroom distribution and use only in the school which has purchased the book, or by the teacher who has purchased the book, and in accordance with the CLA licensing agreement. Photocopying permission is given only for purchasers and not for borrowers of books from any lending service.

Acknowledgements
The publishers gratefully acknowledge permission to reproduce the following copyright material: **AP Watt Ltd** for the use of illustrations from *Revolting Rhymes* by Roald Dahl illustrated by Quentin Blake, Illustrations © 1982, 1984, 2001 Quentin Blake (1982, Jonathan Cape). **David Higham Associates** for the use of extracts from *Revolting Rhymes* by Roald Dahl © 1982, Roald Dahl (1982, Jonathan Cape. **Penguin Group Ltd** for the use of the front cover of *Revolting Rhymes* by Roald Dahl and illustrated by Quentin Blake (1984, 2001, Puffin Books). Text © 1982 Roald Dahl Nominee Ltd. Illustrations © 1982, 1984, 2001, Quentin Blake. Every effort has been made to trace copyright holders for the works reproduced in this book, and the publishers apologise for any inadvertent omissions.

Revolting Rhymes

About the book

Fairy tales that explore similar themes exist in a variety of cultures. They have a strong oral tradition, which continued even after tales were recorded in literary form, mainly in the 18th and 19th centuries. Fairy tales tend to be read to children rather than by them, thus continuing the oral tradition. Children listen, imagining scenes as they unfold and join in with the refrains, becoming partners in the repeated narrative.

The children's books of Roald Dahl evoke a similar response. In many of his books for children, Dahl employs the form of fairy tales. The world his characters inhabit is one with which we can readily identify, but one in which strange and mysterious things can happen. The characters are stereotypical, often grotesque, and are capable of inflicting great mental and physical violence upon their victims, who are usually children. In the end, the oppressed invariably triumph over their adult tormentors.

Revolting Rhymes is a gift for any teacher as it enables a focus on the entertaining as well as the educative aspects of teaching. It consists of six well-known fairy tales, each having been given a new, humorous twist. The language is modern and direct. Dahl does not hesitate to employ colloquialism or even slang – sometimes to quite shocking effect! Because of this, the tales demand to be performed, not just read.

His characters are more complicated than those found in traditional tales. Cinderella becomes not merely a put-upon drudge, but a calculating man-hunter, who not only has a good idea of what she wants out of life, but knows exactly how she is going to achieve it.

Snow-White shows that she is a modern girl who displays more than enough initiative and courage to enable her to make her way in the world. In 'Goldilocks', the narrator would bring criminal charges against the thoughtless anti-heroine. The apparently feckless Jack, once rid of his domineering mother, cures his personal hygiene problem and becomes a millionaire. Little Red Riding Hood becomes an upper-class 'material girl' as well as a cold-blooded killer. Fairy-tale worlds merge when she is invited into the story of 'The Three Little Pigs'. Expected to save the day, she surprises us all, but especially Little Pig!

About the author

Roald Dahl was born in Llandaff, Wales in 1916 to Norwegian parents. His early working life was spent in East Africa, working for the Shell Petroleum Company. He joined the Royal Air Force in 1939 and flew Hurricanes in action in Greece.

Dahl became famous in the late 1940s as a writer of both adult and children's books. He did his writing in a small hut at the bottom of his garden and first began working with illustrator Quentin Blake in 1976. Their partnership continued throughout Dahl's career, until his death in November 1990.

Facts and figures

Revolting Rhymes was first published in 1982. The following year, his book *The Witches* won the Whitbread Award and, in 1988, he won the Children's Book Award for *Matilda*. Roald Dahl's work has been translated into a total of 34 languages.

Guided reading

Before reading

Before you begin to read *Revolting Rhymes*, discuss the characteristics of fairy tales with the children. A shared understanding of what constitutes the original form is essential in understanding the parody.

Talk about the common features and themes of fairy tales, such as magic, good and evil, the transforming power of love and the seemingly ordinary being extraordinary. Ask the children: *What type of characters do we meet?* (Giants, witches, trolls, princes and princesses.) *What are the settings we associate with fairy tales?* (Forests and woods in lands far, far away.) Dwellings are either humble or grand – woodcutters' cottages or palaces and castles. Beginnings and endings are prescribed and predictable: *Once upon a time…* invariably leads to *…and they all lived happily ever after.*

Move on to reminding children of the traditional tales included in *Revolting Rhymes* by reading them together or watching a film. Now try one or more of these ideas:
- Ask the children to recount short parts of narrative in sequence in storytelling circles.
- Challenge groups to split the story into several parts, with each group member writing and illustrating one or two parts on separate pages of a flipchart.
- Invite groups to produce a PowerPoint presentation of the traditional tale.
- Ask groups to divide the story into parts, with each group member designing a separate page that can be made into a big zigzag book.
- These groups could also dramatise a scene from a story. Encourage the children to constructively comment upon and improve other groups' performances.
- Ask the children to gather and compare several versions of the same tale.

Generic guided reading

The stories in *Revolting Rhymes* must be introduced to the children with a performance by the teacher. Rehearse this first, paying close attention to punctuation and savouring the animated, spirited language. Mark the occasional changes to the easy rhythm (iambic tetrameter).

Following your performance, encourage the children to recount the new tale around the class to check their understanding. Discuss any differences between the traditional and 'revolting' versions.

Clap the rhythm of a tale to establish that there are eight beats in most lines. (All tales have the same pattern.) Draw the children's attention to examples of breaks in the normal rhythm. Can the children explain why Dahl does this? (To heighten the dramatic effect; to draw attention to important events; to echo traditional refrains.)

There are rhyming couplets in every tale. Can the children spot exceptions to this pattern? (The pattern is occasionally changed, and for the same reasons as the changes in rhythm.)

Cinderella

The traditional voice of the narrator is gentle, kindly and loving. Ask the children in what ways this narrator is different. (He appears to dislike children, is superior and knows something we don't.) Point out the significance of punctuation. For example, in line two, the short sentence *You don't* is strong and commanding.

Ask: *At what point did you first know that this is a very different story?* Read the first lines, drawing attention to the conversational style, the use of slang and the Americanism, *guess.*

Explain what an anachronism is – something that is historically out of place. Challenge the children to find examples in the story. (The Disco, panty-hose, loo that flushes and so on.) Can the children explain the affect of anachronisms? (They are amusing.)

When Cinderella is introduced, ask: *How did you know she was very different from traditional character?* (She bellows, has a tantrum, is demanding and materialistic – she is clearly chasing the Prince.)

Ask: *What lesson are we taught by this fairy story?* (Wealth doesn't make us happy.) Do the children agree with this moral?

Guided reading

Jack and the Beanstalk

Ask the children to describe the terrifying events that occur during the story. (Jack is beaten with a vacuum cleaner handle for half an hour; Jack meets a terrible giant; his mum is eaten by the giant.) Can they explain how Dahl makes us laugh rather than gasp in horror at these incidents? (The exaggerated nature of the events; the casual language and slang used to describe what happens; the inappropriate response to these events by the characters involved.)

How does Dahl show us what Jack thinks when his mother is eaten? (The use of comic language such as *by Christopher* and *by gum*.) What are the only words Jack says about his dead mum? (*I had a hunch that she was smelly*.) Discuss why Jack doesn't care about his mum.

Encourage the children to explain why the lesson being taught by this story makes us laugh. (Taking a daily bath in case a giant smells and eats you is an absurd idea.) Explore the reasons why it actually *is* a good idea to keep clean.

Snow-White and the Seven Dwarfs

Draw the children's attention to the section of the rhyme from *Now every day, week in week out* to *And you can bet your life she did*. Ask the children to report on examples of the modern language, the very relaxed vocabulary and the conversational style. (There are many examples, including *spoiled and stupid; you are the cat's pyjamas; silly Queen; yelled; I'll cook her flaming goose* and so on.) Ask: *What effect does this language have on us?* (We gasp in amazement; we gasp in horror; it makes us laugh.) Ask: *Why does it affect us in this way?* (We know what to expect of the language and style of fairy stories and it is the surprise of the modern slang that is amusing.)

Now point out the way in which the characters speak and the language they use. (For example, *scrag that child; slit her ribs apart; beat it, kid*.) Ask: *What sort of characters in films and books speak in this way?* (Gangsters.)

Ask: *What is the moral of this tale?* (Gambling is acceptable, so long as you win.) Do the children agree with this? Is this another of Dahl's jokes?

Goldilocks and the Three Bears

Ask the children to identify the line in which the narrator says whose side he is on in the tale: *About a brazen little crook*. Can they see what narrator's tricks are used to pull us onto his side? (The narrator builds sympathy for the bears by describing in great detail what excellent creatures they are.) Draw the children's attention to the rhetorical questions (these do not have an answer but are used to persuade us): *How would you feel if…?* Can the children recognise how we are called upon to use our imagination? (*Now just imagine how* you'd *feel…*)

Challenge the children to identify some of the words used to describe Goldilocks (*toad, louse*). Explain that these are metaphors (figures of speech that say a person doesn't only look or behave like something else but actually *is* something else).

Focus on the scene in the bed and the build-up of the unpleasant description of Goldilocks' shoes. Can they identify the final horror? (Dog poo!) Ask the children to explain what effect this line has on us. (It makes us shudder and laugh out loud at the same time.)

Little Red Riding Hood

Encourage the children to explain why the opening scene is funny rather than horrific. (The conversational, matter-of-fact statements that describe the dramatic situation have an amusing effect; there is no terrifying imagery; she is eaten in *one big bite*.)

Draw the children's attention to the lines from *He quickly put on Grandma's clothes* to *Then sat himself in Grandma's chair*. Ask: *What effect does this detailed preparation have on the reader?* (It builds dramatic tension in anticipation of Little Red Riding Hood's visit.)

Guided reading

The Three Little Pigs

Draw the children's attention to the way we are drawn into the fantasy of this story. The narrator asks us, chummily, what we would think if we saw a pig building a house of straw. The stress is upon the absurdity of the straw and not upon the pig building a house. Point out that the narrator is asking us to suspend belief in a big way and we step right in!

Ask the children to comment on the style of the narrator. Who is he? (The narrator talks about courtesy, strolling through the woods and nobility, which is the language of a gentleman.) Are the children able to give examples of the slang that contrasts with this language? (*I really dig; That pig has had his chips.*)

Invite the children to identify similarities to the original tale. (The refrain, *Little pig,*

little pig...)

Draw their attention to the slaughter of the second little pig and ask the children to describe the character of the wolf. (Greedy, savage, lacking pity.) Point out that the wolf has been anthropomorphised (or humanised – can speak and think).

Looking at the line *So creeping quietly as a mouse*, ask: *What figure of speech is this and is it effective?* (It is a simile that is effective because it emphasises the contrast between mouse and wolf, at the same time stressing the silence of movement.)

Point out the lines from *The wolf stood there...* to *...dripping from his jaw.* Ask the children what is different about this language. (The dramatic change from chatty to threatening and vivid. The wolf is real and no longer anthropomorphic.) What will happen to Little Red Riding Hood?

Shared reading

Extract 1

● Underline the verbs in this extract that are substituted for *said*. (*Screamed, muttered, roared, yelled, cried, replied*.) From these verbs, identify the three that build an atmosphere of noise and hysteria. Circle the other verbs that create a scene of frantic action. (*Chopped, whack, swung, smack, crashing, bounced, rolled, bouncing, torn, chops*.) Explain that this chaotic scene is the climax of the story and also the turning point – Cinderella's change of heart.

● Point out to the class that the hysteria builds to fever pitch and then comes down to a quiet moment before building up again. Underline two pauses in the madness (*He muttered, 'Let me out of here.'* and *He smiled and said, 'She's prettier without her head.'*).

● Circle the line that signals a change of scene from high madness to the ordinary happenings of the day. (*In the kitchen, peeling spuds*.) Explain that the literary device of sudden switches from high drama to the mundane is called bathos. Ask: *How does the use of bathos affect the reader?* (It makes us laugh.)

Extract 2

● Explain to the children that the narrator uses language generally found in speech, rather than in writing. This is called colloquial language. Circle examples of colloquial words and phrases in the last six lines of the extract. (*My sainted souls, gape, clot, grab the lot, scrambled*.) Ask: *How does colloquial language affect the reader?* (The narrator has a conversational style, making us feel that the story is being told to us. Because the language is unexpected and inappropriate, it makes us laugh.)

● Underline the names that Mum calls Jack. (*Crazy boy, chump, lunatic, little clot*.) Establish that this use of language demonstrates what Mum thinks of Jack. Circle two events that show how little she cares for her son. (She beats him and sends him up the towering beanstalk.)

● Underline the words *vacuum-cleaner, Mini* and *Rolls*. Ask: *Why do we laugh when these are mentioned?* (They come from the modern age and didn't exist in the time of 'Jack and the Beanstalk'.) Explain that they are called anachronisms.

Extract 3

● Circle the first three sentences. Discuss the way in which these short statements and one-syllable words build suspense.

● Underline the only two lines in the next verse that scan in the usual rhythm: *'What great big ears you have, Grandma'* and *'What great big eyes you have, Grandma'*. Point out that the complete disruption of rhythm caused by the other lines halts the easy flow of language and heightens the dramatic effect.

● Discuss the clever humour of the lines *'That's wrong!' cried Wolf. 'Have you forgot, To tell me what BIG TEETH I've got?'* (The Wolf doesn't like this departure from the traditional story.)

● Clap the syllables in the line *The small girl smiles. One eyelid flickers.* and point out that the transformation of Red Riding Hood is marked by a change in rhythm.

● Explain to the children that *eyelid flickers* could be a wink. Ask: *What effect does the risqué word 'knickers' have?* (It adds to our amusement.)

● Ask: *What does the final line tell us about the character of Red Riding Hood?* (She is self-interested and practical, but also fashionable and materialistic.)

Extract 1

Cinderella

Thousands of eager people came
To try it on, but all in vain.
Now came the Ugly Sisters' go.
One tried it on. The Prince screamed, 'No!'
But she screamed, 'Yes! It fits! Whoopee!
'So now you've got to marry me!'
The Prince went white from ear to ear.
He muttered, 'Let me out of here.'
'Oh no you don't! You made a vow!'
'There's no way you can back out now!'
'Off with her head!' the Prince roared back.
They chopped it off with one big whack.
This pleased the Prince. He smiled and said,
'She's prettier without her head.'
Then up came Sister Number Two,
Who yelled, 'Now *I* will try the shoe!'
'Try this instead!' the Prince yelled back.
He swung his trusty sword and *smack* –
Her head went crashing to the ground.
It bounced a bit and rolled around.
In the kitchen, peeling spuds,
Cinderella heard the thuds
Of bouncing heads upon the floor,
And poked her own head round the door.
'What's all the racket?' Cindy cried.
'Mind your own bizz,' the Prince replied.
Poor Cindy's heart was torn to shreds.
My Prince! She thought. He chops off *heads*!
How could I marry anyone
Who does that sort of thing for fun?

Text © 1982 Roald Dahl Nominee Ltd; Illustrations © 1982, 1984, 2001 Quentin Blake.

■SCHOLASTIC
www.scholastic.co.uk

Extract 2

Jack and the Beanstalk

'You crazy boy! D'you really mean
'You sold our Daisy for a bean?'
She snatched the bean. She yelled, 'You chump!'
And flung it on the rubbish-dump.
Then summoning up all her power,
She beat the boy for half an hour,
Using (and nothing could be meaner)
The handle of a vacuum-cleaner.
At ten p.m. or thereabout,
The little bean began to sprout.
By morning it had grown so tall
You couldn't see the top at all.
Young Jack cried, 'Mum, admit it now!
'It's better than a rotten cow!'
The mother said, 'You lunatic!
'Where are the beans that I can pick?
'There's not *one bean*! It's bare as bare!'
'No no!' cried Jack. 'You look up there!
'Look very high and you'll behold
'Each single leaf is solid gold!'
By gollikins, the boy was right!
Now, glistening in the morning light,
The mother actually perceives
A mass of lovely golden leaves!
She yells out loud, 'My sainted souls!
'I'll sell the Mini, buy a Rolls!
'Don't stand and gape, you little clot!
'Get up there quick and grab the lot!'
Jack was nimble, Jack was keen,
He scrambled up the mighty bean.

ext © 1982 Roald Dahl Nominee Ltd; Illustrations © 1982, 1984, 2001 Quentin Blake.

Extract 3

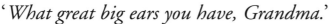

Little Red Riding Hood
In came the little girl in red.
She stopped. She stared. And then she said,

'*What great big ears you have, Grandma.*'
'*All the better to hear you with,*' the Wolf replied.
'*What great big eyes you have, Grandma,*'
        said Little Red Riding Hood.
'*All the better to see you with,*' the Wolf replied.

He sat there watching her and smiled.
He thought, I'm going to eat this child.
Compared with her old Grandmamma
She's going to taste like caviare.

Then Little Red Riding Hood said, '*But Grandma,
what a great big furry coat you have on.*'

'That's wrong!' cried Wolf. 'Have you forgot
To tell me what BIG TEETH I've got?
'Ah well, no matter what you say,
'I'm going to eat you anyway.'
The small girl smiles. One eyelid flickers.
She whips a pistol from her knickers,
She aims it at the creature's head
And *bang, bang, bang,* she shoots him dead.
A few weeks later in the wood,
I came across Miss Riding Hood.
But what a change! No cloak of red,
No silly hood upon her head.
She said, 'Hello, and please do note
'My lovely furry WOLFSKIN COAT.'

ext © 1982 Roald Dahl Nominee Ltd; Illustrations © 1982, 1984, 2001 Quentin Blake.

Plot, character and setting

Spot the difference!

Objective: To make notes on and use evidence from across a text to explain events or ideas.
What you need: Copies of *Revolting Rhymes*, a copy of photocopiable page 15 for each child, writing materials.

What to do

● Read 'Cinderella' to the class and ask the children: *What are the main differences between the traditional tale and the* Revolting Rhymes *version?* (The Prince's character, Cinderella's character, the plot.)
● Discuss the differences you have identified. Point out that it is the extremity of the differences between the well-known tale and this new version that makes us laugh. We are expecting to read the events of the traditional 'Cinderella'

and the shock when they don't transpire, plus the absurdity of the new events, makes us laugh out loud.
● Distribute copies of the book to groups of children and challenge them to make notes that demonstrate these differences with direct reference to the text.
● Using their notes, ask the children to complete photocopiable page 15.

Differentiation
For older/more confident learners: Challenge the children to identify the lines that made them laugh most and explain why to the class.
For younger/less confident learners: Ask the children to identify two differences in the story events.

Getting to know Jack

Objective: To identify and summarise evidence from a text to support a hypothesis.
What you need: Copies of *Revolting Rhymes*, photocopiable page 16, writing materials.

What to do

● Begin by asking the children: *How do we gain information about people's personalities when reading stories?* (Explain that, just as in real life, we know a person by their actions and words, the way they treat others and usually by what others say about them.)
● Read the story of 'Jack and the Beanstalk' with the children and ask: *Why, in the case of Jack, do we not believe the shocking things his mum says about him?* (Dahl has created such a terrible mother that we neither like her nor believe a word she says.)
● Explain that, when commenting upon characters from a story, it is essential to be able

to prove points with reference to the text. Ask the children to re-read the rhyme in groups of three and to note each thing they learn about Jack's character. Next to each point, they should write *I know this because...* and refer to the story for supporting evidence. Discuss the groups' ideas as a class.
● Tell the children that they are now going to use what they have found out about Jack to invent more details about his character. (They will use these ideas in the activity 'A sequel' in Section 5.) Working in their groups, encourage the children to complete photocopiable page 16.

Differentiation
For older/more confident learners: Children can write a character study about Jack, using their group's notes.
For younger/less confident learners: Children can draw pictures or have their ideas scribed by an adult.

Plot, character and setting

The reader/writer partnership

Objective: To compare the usefulness of techniques such as visualisation in exploring the meaning of texts.
What you need: Copies of *Revolting Rhymes*, large sheets of paper, art and writing materials.
Cross-curricular link: Art and design.

What to do

● Explain to the class that when we read, we enter into partnership with the author of the text. The writer trusts that the readers' imaginations will enable us to visualise parts of the story that are not described. Tell the children that you are going to test this theory by creating pictures of the settings in 'Snow-White and the Seven Dwarfs'.
● Read the story with the children and ask: *In what place does the story begin?* (The palace.) Tell the children that as you re-read the tale, they must make a list noting each change of scene.

● Invite them to share their findings and correct their lists. (Palace, forest, butcher's shop, palace, city, race track, palace counting house, palace parlour, mighty hall, home of the seven dwarfs, Barclays Bank, Ascot racetrack.)
● Allocate one scene to each group of two or three children. Invite each group to draw a picture of their scene and to annotate it with carefully chosen nouns and adjectives.
● Display the pictures and read the rhyme again. Discuss the way in which the visualisation adds to enjoyment and understanding of the rhyme.

Differentiation
For older/more confident learners: Encourage the children to write a paragraph of prose, building the atmosphere of their scene.
For younger/less confident learners: Provide the children with nouns and ask them to suggest adjectives.

A new viewpoint

Objective: To vary and develop the viewpoint through the portrayal of action and selection of detail.
What you need: Copies of *Revolting Rhymes*.

What to do

● Begin by asking the children to list the characteristics of any story and write their answers on the whiteboard. (Characters, place/setting, problem, resolution.) Discuss each characteristic in turn, noting the differences between the traditional tale of 'Goldilocks' and the *Revolting Rhymes* version. (The only difference is the resolution, where Goldilocks is eaten.)
● Ask: *If characters, place/setting and problem remain the same, why does Dahl's version seem so different from the traditional tale?* (Every story is told from a certain point of view. It is this that has changed the story.)
● Challenge the children to identify the

traditional point of view (Goldilocks) and the *Revolting Rhymes* point of view (the three bears).
● In groups, ask the children to create their own version of 'Sleeping Beauty', told from the point of view of the twelfth fairy godmother, who was angry because she did not receive an invitation to the christening. They should prepare an oral storytelling of the new version to perform. Only the end of the story plot may be changed – apart from this and the point of view, every aspect of the story will remain the same.

Differentiation
For older/more confident learners: Children can choose their own fairy stories to retell from a new viewpoint. These can be recorded or written down.
For younger/less confident learners: Children can write a list of thoughts going through the godmother's head as she travels to the christening: about the king, queen, other godmothers and finally the baby.

Plot, character and setting

Here come the girls!

> **Objective:** To infer writers' perspectives from what is written and from what is implied.
> **What you need:** Copies of *Revolting Rhymes*, writing materials.

What to do

● Remind the children of the traditional tale of 'Little Red Riding Hood' and point out that, in this version, she is a passive character. (Remind the children that 'passive' means that things happen to the character, or are done to her.)
● Ask the children: *What is different about Little Red Riding Hood's character in the* Revolting Rhymes *version?* (She is in control and more 'pro-active' – she makes decisions and does things that change the direction of the story.)
● Working in groups, invite the children to compile lists of good and bad female characters from fairy tales. Discuss these and re-organise them on the whiteboard under the headings of 'Passive' and 'Pro-active'. (Passive: Rapunzel, Cinderella, Snow-White, Sleeping Beauty. Pro-active: several stepmothers, Ugly Sisters, many witches, twelfth fairy in 'Sleeping Beauty'.)
● Ask: *Are good female characters generally active or passive?* (Passive.) *What about bad female characters?* (Pro-active.) Discuss what message this gives. (Good females will be rewarded for doing as they are told.) Is this is a good message?
● Compile lists of good female characters from modern literature and television and check if they are passive or pro-active. Has there been a recent change in the role of female characters?

> **Differentiation**
> **For older/more confident learners:** Challenge the children to compile similar lists for male fairy-tale characters.
> **For younger/less confident learners:** Provide the children with a list of character names to cut out and stick on the appropriate list.

Vivid events

> **Objective:** To explore how writers use language for comic and dramatic effects.
> **What you need:** Copies of Extract 3, photocopiable page 17.

What to do

● Give groups of children a copy of Extract 3 and explain that Dahl has used a change of tense in this rhyme. Ask: *In what tense has the beginning of the story been written?* (Past.) Point out that while the majority of the story has been told in the past tense, four lines have been written in the present. Challenge groups to find these.
● Check the answer (from *The small girl smiles…* to *…she shoots him dead*). Ask the children individually to rewrite these lines in the past tense. Encourage them to compare past and present tense versions. Ask: *Are the lines as effective in the past tense? Why is this?* (No. The present tense: places a moving picture in the reader's mind; stresses the immediacy of events; impacts vividly upon the reader's imagination.)
● Suggest that for these same reasons, people often describe dramatic incidents that happen in their lives in the present tense. Ask the children to choose one beginning from photocopiable page 17 and complete the story. In groups, allow one minute for each child to recount their adventure. Discuss how effective this technique is for communicating an adventure in a vivid way.

> **Differentiation**
> **For older/more confident learners:** Children can recount present tense personal adventures orally and in writing.
> **For younger/less confident learners:** Create past and present tense story beginning cards that children can sort by tense.

Plot, character and setting

The world of fairy tales

> **Objective:** To explore how writers use language for comic and dramatic effects.
> **What you need:** Copies of *Revolting Rhymes*, writing materials.

What to do

● Read 'The Three Little Pigs' with the class. Challenge the children to give an example from the tale that shows how characters from different fairy tales inhabit the same world. (Little Pig rings Little Red Riding Hood to ask for help.)
● Point out that the four lines in 'Little Red Riding Hood' that describe the killing of the wolf are repeated in 'The Three Little Pigs'. Ask: *What effect does this have?* (We are prepared for what is about to happen next.)
● Read the last six lines of 'The Three Little Pigs' again. Ask: *Why does the ending shock?* (The two characters seemed to be friends.) Discuss

how Dahl prepares us for the twist at the end. Ask: *What is the narrator's attitude to the pigs?* (They are silly – the use of the diminutive *piglet* enhances the condescending attitude.)
● Look at the formal language used in these lines. (*Young ladies, upper crust, Miss Riding Hood, one notes.*) Suggest that this switch to formal language emphasises the comedy of the double-cross.
● Challenge groups of children to develop an oral storyline in which the three Billy Goats Gruff call on the help of Miss Riding Hood. What twist might occur at the end?

> **Differentiation**
> **For older/more confident learners:** Children can explore swaps of character between other stories.
> **For younger/less confident learners:** Children can draw the fate of the troll on one half of paper and the fate of the goats on the other half, adding sentences to describe the scenes.

Anthropomorphism in action

> **Objective:** To infer writers' perspectives from what is written and from what is implied.
> **What you need:** Copies of *Revolting Rhymes*, photocopiable page 18, writing and drawing materials.

What to do

● Encourage the children to give examples from fairy tales of animals with human characteristics. (Pigs, wolves, bears, goats and so on.) Explain that when storytellers and cartoonists attribute the behaviour or form of human beings to animals, this is called anthropomorphism.
● Working in groups, ask half of the children to read and note their own adjectives to describe the wolf as portrayed in 'The Three Little Pigs' and half to read and make notes on the wolf in 'Little Red Riding Hood'. (Solitary, pitiless, merciless, greedy, self-indulgent, sly, cunning and so on.)
● Invite children to share vocabulary and ask:

What are the differences between the two wolves in these rhymes? (It could be the same wolf.)
● Discuss the negative way that the portrayal of the wolf makes us feel about the species. (This idea is developed further in the activity 'Friend or foe?' in Section 6.)
● Ask the children to complete the activity on photocopiable page 18, and then draw a picture and write a character description of their anthropomorphised animal.

> **Differentiation**
> **For older/more confident learners:** Inspire children to write stories featuring their character. Several characters could be joined in a new world of animal adventures, co-authored in collaborative writing groups.
> **For younger/less confident learners:** Encourage children to draw a picture of their animal and annotate it with human characteristics copied from the photocopiable sheet.

Plot, character and setting

Spot the difference!

● Think about the differences between the traditional tale of 'Cinderella' and the *Revolting Rhymes* version. Write down the exact words from the new tale that show each difference. The first one is done for you.

In the traditional tale…	In the Revolting Rhymes version…
The Prince did not carry a sword.	He swung his trusty sword and *smack* – Her head went crashing to the ground.
The shoe tried on by hopeful girls was a tiny glass slipper.	
When running from the ball, Cinderella *only* left behind a glass slipper.	
The lost slipper was placed on a satin cushion.	
At the beginning of the story, Cinderella was a quiet, sweet, undemanding girl.	
The lesson we learn from the tale is that we should love and care for other people.	

Plot, character and setting

Getting to know Jack

● Imagine that Jack has moved to your school and sits next to you in class. Answer the questions, then draw and write a description of Jack on the back of this sheet.

1. What aspects of schoolwork would Jack be best at?

_____

How do you know this?_____

_____

2. What sport would Jack be good at? _____

I know this because… _____

_____

3. Would Jack be well-behaved? _____

I know this because… _____

_____

4. If challenged by a school bully, would Jack be frightened? _____

I know this because… _____

_____

5. What would you give Jack for his birthday? _____

Why? _____

_____

SCHOLASTIC
www.scholastic.co.uk

Plot, character and setting

Vivid events

● Choose one of these beginnings and continue the story. Remember to use the present tense.

I'm coming down this hill on my bike – too fast. I try to stop. The brakes aren't working…

I hear all this shouting and I race round the corner. There's this huge bully from the top class picking on…

I fall on a broken bottle – there's blood everywhere! I shout for help…

Lightning is flashing. I cover my ears. I dread the roar of the thunder. Rain is…

I scream for help but no sound comes out. I can't run any more. The place is deserted…

Illustrations © 2010, Mike Phillips/Beehive Illustration.

SECTION 4

Anthropomorphism in action

● Writers, cartoonists and film-makers sometimes give human attributes to objects or soft toys – for example, the magic mirror in 'Snow-White and the Seven Dwarfs'. This is also called anthropomorphism. Can you think of three more examples from books, films or cartoons?

Title of story/ cartoon/film	Name of character	Is the character good or evil?

● Think of an animal you know a lot about. What human characteristics would you give to this animal if you were to anthropomorphise it in a story?

Name of animal: _____

Species of animal: _____

● Circle the best words to describe the character and attitudes of your animal:

old   young   bossy   careful   cheerful   miserable   greedy
hard-working   lazy   deceitful   proud   jealous   clever   organised
tidy   messy   timid   sly   leader   friendly   fussy   carefree

What sports would your animal like? _____

Which hobbies would it enjoy? _____

As a character in a book, film or cartoon, would your animal be good or evil?

_____

www.scholastic.co.uk

Talk about it

Reciting the rhymes

Objective: To choose and prepare poems or stories for performance.
What you need: Copies of *Revolting Rhymes*.

What to do
● Explain to the class that *Revolting Rhymes* are best enjoyed when they are recited out loud and particularly when they are shared with an audience.
● To maximise your enjoyment of any of the rhymes for recital, divide it into six parts and distribute to six groups. Challenge the children to read the words with expression and relish. Remind them that the punctuation in a written text gives the instructions for the way in which the words are to be spoken. Punctuation must be *read*. Ask: *When we are reading, what does a full stop tell us to do?* Revise the functions of other punctuation marks in this way.

● Clap the rhythm of a sample of lines. Point out that there are generally eight syllables or beats in every line and that this rhythm needs to be emphasised during the recital. Draw the children's attention to the lines that are the exception. Ask: *Why is the normal rhythm sometimes changed?* (These lines have special importance and Dahl does this to draw attention to them.)
● When the children have rehearsed their lines, invite each group to perform in turn. Ask: *In what ways did the punctuation help with your performance?* Encourage discussion.

Differentiation
For older/more confident learners: Challenge the children to explain the meaning of lines that break normal rhythm.
For younger/less confident learners: Allocate a short extract and give adult support in preparation for recital.

The scene of the crime

Objective: To create roles showing how behaviour can be interpreted from different viewpoints.
What you need: Copies of *Revolting Rhymes*, copies of Extract 1, photocopiable page 22.
Cross-curricular link: Drama.

What to do
● Read the tale of 'Cinderella' to the class. Explain that you are going to imagine that when people hear of the beheading of the sisters there is a public outcry. As a result of the fuss, the Palace agrees to conduct an inquiry into the incident.
● Organise the children into groups of six and distribute copies of Extract 1. Challenge each group to recreate the crime scene as part of the investigation. There are six roles: the Prince, Cinderella, two ugly sisters, a guard and a servant. Explain that the words that are spoken and the way in which they are delivered by four of the characters must be taken from the sheet.

The two new characters need to improvise their lines. Discuss what they may have said during the incident.
● Give the children 20 minutes to rehearse. The crime scenes can then be presented to the inquiry team by each group in turn. At the end of each replay, the class (acting as inquiry team) must ask questions of characters in order to clarify exactly what each character heard and saw. Encourage the children to comment on the quality of the productions using photocopiable page 22. You can develop this idea further by completing the 'Bloggers speak out' activity in Section 6.

Differentiation
For older/more confident learners: Children can write up their dramas as playscripts, observing the conventions.
For younger/less confident learners: Present a playscript to the children and support them in their first few readings.

Talk about it

A sequel

Objective: To use settings and characterisation to engage readers' interest.
What you need: Completed copies of photocopiable page 16, photocopiable page 23.

What to do

● Explain to the children that they are going to create a sequel to 'Jack and the Beanstalk'. Establish that the sequel will be written in prose and in traditional fairy-tale language.
● Remind the children that they have already met Jack and know him quite well. Revise their ideas from their completed photocopiable sheets. Now ask them to imagine that their new friend, Jack, tells them the secret of the beanstalk and asks them to climb the beanstalk with him.
● Children can complete photocopiable page 23 in groups of three as preparation. Explain that, although they will think of ideas together,

they will actually develop and write the story individually. Give them a few minutes to jot down their ideas, and then ask each group to share their best idea with the class.
● Discuss some of the ideas and challenge the children to think about the story sequel overnight. They don't need to stick with the ideas from this session. Nothing must be written down. The story must be told the next day in the oral tradition of storytelling. The next activity explains how the stories will be told.

Differentiation
For older/more confident learners: Children preparing longer or more complex story ideas may want to make notes or sketches to help them tell their stories.
For younger/less confident learners: An adult should establish firm story ideas, using the photocopiable sheet, before the children go home.

Telling the story sequel

Objective: To tell stories effectively and convey detailed information coherently for listeners.
What you need: Preparatory notes and illustrations from the previous activity.

What to do

● Remind the children that their sequels to 'Jack and the Beanstalk' are to be told in traditional fairy-tale style and they should *not* try to make them amusing. Explain that Roald Dahl was a very experienced writer and that he used literary conventions (bathos, anachronisms, colloquial speech) that young writers will learn to use when they are older.
● Invite one child to tell their story sequel to the class. Choose a person who you know will have a good story ready. Model the way in which listeners can improve this story by asking pertinent questions that enable the storyteller to clarify any parts that are confusing. Listeners

may also make suggestions to improve the story.
● Repeat this exercise with a second storyteller and encourage more children to ask questions.
● Organise the children to work with writing partners. They should take turns to listen to one another's stories, ask helpful questions and give useful advice. Allow three minutes for each storytelling and questioning session.
● Encourage the children to comment on the support they were given by their partners.
● The activity 'A beanstalk book' in Section 6 explains how children can finish this project by writing and publishing their stories.

Differentiation
For older/more confident learners: Advise children to extend their stories by inserting pieces of description to create atmosphere.
For younger/less confident learners: Give the children a selection of improvements to their storylines, from which they can choose.

Talk about it

The persuasive seven

Objective: To analyse the use of persuasive language.
What you need: Copies of *Revolting Rhymes*.
Cross-curricular link: Drama.

What to do

● Read the story of 'Snow-White and the Seven Dwarfs' and point out the section where Snow-White finds refuge with the dwarfs in the city.
● Organise the children into groups of five and ask them to work out a short drama in which four of them persuade Snow-White to come and work for them for nothing. Each dwarf should take on a different characteristic that is reflected in what they say. These could match the names given to the dwarfs in the Disney film (Doc, Dopey, Sneezy, Happy, Bashful, Grumpy, Sleepy) or children could invent their own. Snow-White must respond to the persuasion, eventually agreeing.

● Compile a list and discuss the conventions we use when trying to persuade:
  ● Hyperbola: *A wonderfully life-enhancing experience, offering fabulous opportunities…*
  ● Rhetorical questions: *Where else would you find such a jolly group of people to work for?*
  ● Repetition: *Snow-White, you must, I repeat, MUST consider your safety.*
  ● Bribery: *When we win at the races, we will give you chocolates and flowers.*
● Ask the groups to perform their dramas to the class. The other children can give feedback.

Differentiation
For older/more confident learners: Challenge children to write up their dramas as playscripts.
For younger/less confident learners: Provide a set of cards featuring persuasive arguments, from which children can choose.

Guilty or not guilty?

Objective: To develop viewpoint through the portrayal of action and selection of detail.
What you need: Copies of *Revolting Rhymes*, copies of photocopiable page 24.

What to do

● Read the *Revolting Rhymes* version of 'Goldilocks' to the children and encourage them to select examples from the text that demonstrate from which characters' point of view it is told. (The narrator calls Goldilocks a *brazen little crook, little toad* and worse as the tale unfolds. He writes from the point of view of the bears.)
● Now ask the children: *From what point of view is the traditional tale told?* Read the tale if necessary and establish that, though sympathetic to Goldilocks, the traditional version gives no explanation as to why a young girl might be driven to seek refuge in a stranger's house. (Is she running away, escaping or being chased?)

Organise the children into groups of five and ask them to come up with as many ideas as possible to complete photocopiable page 24.
● Encourage the groups to develop their own stories, narrated from the point of view of Goldilocks. Suggest that they fill in details, explaining why Goldilocks is so desperate and justifying her actions. Using brief notes of the storyline to help them, they can tell their new stories to the rest of the class. Compare the new stories and the *Revolting Rhymes* version. Is Goldilocks guilty or not guilty?

Differentiation
For older/more confident learners: Children can create a court drama, using points developed for the prosecution and the defence.
For younger/less confident learners: Complete two or three alternative answers on the photocopiable sheet and ask the children to choose which to use in their stories.

Talk about it

The scene of the crime

● Use this sheet to evaluate how well each group recreates the crime scene from 'Cinderella'. Grade each aspect of performance on a scale from 1 to 5, with 5 being excellent.

The title of the performance made you want to watch and find out more.

The actors spoke clearly and confidently.

It was easy to hear the actors.

The actors did not turn their backs on the audience.

The actors spoke their lines with appropriate expression.

The actions on the stage helped to make the story clear.

The audience knew when to clap because the end was clear.

One piece of advice I would like to offer the actors is…

_____

_____

_____

One piece of advice I would like to offer the playwright is…

_____

_____

_____

A sequel

● Imagine that Jack is going to climb the beanstalk again and has asked you to go with him. What happens next? For each question, think quickly and fill in three completely different ideas.

Why does Jack want to climb the beanstalk again?

1. _____

2. _____

3. _____

What is the land like at the top of the beanstalk?

1. _____

2. _____

3. _____

What danger do you encounter?

1. _____

2. _____

3. _____

What ordinary thing do you have in your pocket that will help you deal with the danger?

1. _____

2. _____

3. _____

How do you manage to get back down the beanstalk?

1. _____

2. _____

3. _____

Illustrations © 2010, Mike Phillips/Beehive Illustration.

PHOTOCOPIABLE

Talk about it

SECTION 5

Guilty or not guilty?

● In *Revolting Rhymes*, Goldilocks is accused of three crimes. Put together the case for her defence and think of reasons why she acted as she did. Write three different answers to each question below.

Crime one: Breaking and entering someone's house
Why is a young girl seeking refuge in a house in the woods?

1. _____

2. _____

3. _____

Crime two: Stealing a bowl of porridge
Why is she starving?

1. _____

2. _____

3. _____

Crime three: Breaking Baby Bear's precious chair
Why does she need to sit down and rest?

1. _____

2. _____

3. _____

Crime four: Ruining Baby Bear's sheets
Why is she so desperately tired that she falls asleep in a strange house with her shoes on?

1. _____

2. _____

3. _____

PHOTOCOPIABLE

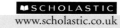

www.scholastic.co.uk

READ & RESPOND: Activities based on *Revolting Rhymes*

Get writing

Bloggers speak out

Objective: To summarise and shape material and ideas from different sources to write convincing and informative non-narrative texts.
What you need: A copy of photocopiable page 28 for each child, access to computers.
Cross-curricular links: Citizenship, ICT.

What to do

● This activity follows on from 'The scene of the crime' in Section 5. After the re-enactments, the Inquiry Team has published its report.
● Discuss what children understand about blogging. (Writing personal opinions about any subject online. The style is conversational and informal.) Explain that adults make their political views known by blogging. When government reports are published there are thousands of blogs, written by ordinary people, stating opinions for and against the report.

● Distribute copies of photocopiable page 28 and read the text aloud. Discuss the children's responses and explain that they are going to write a personal blog outlining their views. Remind them that this is a dangerous activity. This government won't like opposition and they will need to be brave. Explain that they are responding as citizens of the kingdom and not as the characters they played in the re-enactment.
● Ask the children to highlight points in the report with which they disagree. They should then go through these one at a time, stating their opinions. They can word-process their blogs.

Differentiation
For older/more confident learners: Ask the children to also write formal letters of protest to the Palace.
For younger/less confident learners: Children can work in a group with adult support to read the report.

A beanstalk book

Objective: To reflect independently and critically on their own writing and edit and improve it.
What you need: Copies of *Revolting Rhymes*, a thin jotter for each child, sheets of A3 cartridge paper, writing and art materials.
Cross-curricular links: Design and technology, art and design.

What to do

● Explain to the children that they will now be writing, editing and publishing their sequels to 'Jack and the Beanstalk' (from Section 5).
● Tell the children that Roald Dahl wrote his rough notes for story characters, settings and ideas in a jotter that he called his 'Story ideas book'. Explain to the class that, like Dahl, they will write rough drafts in their own story ideas books.
● Give each child a jotter and encourage them to make notes and draft ideas, scoring out mistakes

and changes and moving pieces of text by circling chunks and using arrows to reposition them.
● Cut sheets of A3 cartridge paper in half, lengthways, and fold these strips into zigzag books. Tell the children that the finished stories will be written *down* the strip, enabling the storybook to unfold. Extra strips may be added to make very long books for enthusiastic writers.
● Working with their writing partners, encourage the children to support each other as they edit, re-draft and illustrate. Organise a book launch for parents to visit, read and review the books.

Differentiation
For older/more confident learners: Encourage children to write extended stories with additional pieces of dialogue or description.
For younger/less confident learners: Give children additional adult and peer support, including scribing where necessary.

Get writing

The Queen transformed

Objective: To experiment with different narrative form and styles to write their own stories.
What you need: Copies of *Revolting Rhymes*, photocopiable page 29, writing materials.

What to do
● Remind the children that we get to know what people and book characters are like by seeing what others say about them, the things they say, how they speak and the things they do.
● Re-read the story of 'Snow-White and the Seven Dwarves' down to *Oh where, oh where had Snow-White gone?* Ask the children to listen or to read carefully, searching for the clues that tell them about the Queen. They can then complete the first half of photocopiable page 29.
● Explain that characters sometimes change from being evil to being good – for example, the Selfish Giant, Hansel and Gretel's father, and Kay in 'The Snow Queen'. This transformation comes about when something happens to make them realise how bad they have been.
● Discuss ideas for what could happen in the life of Miss Maclahose (the Queen) to transform her to a good character – perhaps the loss of the power of the mirror, the loss of Snow-White, or maybe she gets a pet who melts her heart. Ask the children to complete the second half of the sheet with information about the transformed character. Children can use these notes to write a new ending, in traditional prose, for the story of 'Snow-White'.

Differentiation
For older/more confident learners: Challenge children to identify and analyse transformed characters in other stories.
For younger/less confident learners: Highlight clues about the character of the Queen in the text.

A missing girl

Objective: To compare different types of information texts and identify how they are structured.
What you need: Copies of *Revolting Rhymes*, a copy of photocopiable page 30 for each child, writing materials, access to computers (optional).
Cross-curricular link: ICT.

What to do
● Read the story of 'Goldilocks and the Three Bears' and tell the children that they are now reporters for the Daily Magic Mirror. Their job is to investigate and write a newspaper report on the mysterious disappearance of local girl, Goldilocks.
● Establish that the first sentence of a newspaper report always answers the Five 'W's: Where? When? Who? What? Why? List the answers to these questions on the whiteboard. (The Three Bears' cottage; yesterday morning; Goldilocks; went missing; don't know yet.)
● Challenge children individually to write one sentence that includes all this information in any order they choose. Discuss their results.
● Explain that the rest of such a report will give more information about each of the 'W's and will include quotations from people who have been interviewed. Children can use the notes on photocopiable page 30 to get them started.
● Check the children know that the headline for a newspaper report must be eye-catching, short and should sum up the main message of the report. Encourage suggestions and then set the children to work writing their reports on paper or on the computer.

Differentiation
For older/more confident learners: Challenge children to invent their own conclusion and quotes by a wide range of characters.
For younger/less confident learners: Children can base their reports on the notes provided.

Get writing

The essence of fairy-tale animals

> **Objective:** To adapt non-narrative forms and styles to write fiction or factual texts, including poems.
> **What you need:** Copies of *Revolting Rhymes* and other fairy tales, writing materials.

What to do
- Write the following poem on the whiteboard:
    Frightened squealer
    Flat-snouted snuffler
    Dainty two-toed trotter
    Greedy grunter
    Comic snorter
    Mud roller
    Curly tailed befriender
    PIG
- Read the poem and invite comments on the layout. (Long, thin shape, very few words.) Elicit that this is a list of physical characteristics and actions that sum up the essence of a pig.

- Tell the children that they are going to try this for another fairy-tale animal: the bear. Write a list of suitable verbs (*roar, growl, hunt,* and so on).
- Explain that we can change these verbs to nouns by adding the suffix 'er'. Demonstrate this on the board (*roarer, growler, hunter*). Point out that this list sums up the essence of the bear, rather than describing what it does.
- Encourage the children to provide apt adjectives to describe these nouns – *mighty roarer, threatening growler, stealthy hunter, savage ripper, winter sleeper, great bear.*
- Ask children in small groups to repeat the process to sum up the essence of a wolf.

> **Differentiation**
> **For older/more able learners:** Children can compose poems about other fairy-tale animals.
> **For younger/less confident learners:** Provide a list of 'wolf' verbs – howl, stalk, prowl, pounce, stare.

Friend or foe?

> **Objective:** To establish, balance and maintain viewpoints in non-narrative texts.
> **What you need:** A2 poster paper, writing materials, access to the internet, information books on wolves.
> **Cross-curricular links:** ICT, science.

What to do
- Tell the children that wolves in Scotland were hunted to extinction 250 years ago. The Wolf Trust wants to reintroduce the wolf to the Highlands of Scotland, but it faces opposition. Invite them to comment.
- Ask: *Why do you think wolves have such a bad reputation?* Establish that fairy tales have contributed to their fearsome reputation.
- Tell the children that they are going to write an informed discussion about the points for and against returning the wild wolf to Scotland. Working in groups, they should divide a sheet of A2 paper in half lengthways and, using research

from the internet and books, write a numbered list of arguments down each half of the paper.
- Invite the children to discuss with their groups the personal opinion that they have reached on the issue. Encourage them to listen carefully and be prepared to change their minds.
- Display the groups' lists of arguments and explain that they must now each write one paragraph explaining the advantages of re-introducing the wolf, one paragraph against and a final paragraph in which they state and explain their conclusions on the subject.

> **Differentiation**
> **For older/more confident learners:** Encourage children to add their views as blogs on your school website.
> **For younger/less confident learners:** Put children into pairs, with one child writing a paragraph for reintroducing wolves, the other writing a paragraph against and then a joint conclusion.

Bloggers speak out

Inquiry report into the deaths of the Ugly Sisters under suspicious circumstances

People on the inquiry team

People chosen by the Prince to be on the inquiry team are all honest citizens. Only two of them (the King and Queen) are actually related to the Prince and they would never allow this to influence their decisions. Five of the team members have recently moved into large mansions and have given up work. This is pure coincidence and any person who says that these excellent citizens were paid to agree with the King about the crime will suffer the same fate as those two ugly birds.

Process of the inquiry

The team interviewed all witnesses who were at the crime scene. Several people who knew the Ugly Sisters were asked to give evidence about their characters. (Newspapers that reported that these were enemies of the Ugly Sisters have been closed down.) The inquiry team saw a re-enactment of the crime scene to ensure that they were clear about the circumstances surrounding our dear Prince's dreadful experience.

Report

Our dear, beloved Prince is of course absolutely innocent of any crime. He has been stalked for many years by these Ugly Sisters. People who hate the Ugly Sisters have come forward to say that they have been plotting to marry the Prince and take over the kingdom.

Cinderella was looking beautiful on the day of the inquiry and our generous, sweet Prince even offered to marry her in compensation for the loss of her two sisters. The stupid girl replied that she needed to get home to her husband and their jam-making business.

That is the end of the matter and no more will be said about this. Be warned that any citizens caught marching or blogging in protest about this report will be imprisoned.

PHOTOCOPIABLE

www.scholastic.co.uk

The Queen transformed

● Complete the first column of the table with information about the character of the Queen in the story of 'Snow-White and the Seven Dwarfs'.

● In the second column, write down how we would know that the Queen was now a good character if a new story was written about her.

● What is the event that transforms the Queen from an evil character to a good character?

	Queen's character in the story	Queen's transformed character
What does the narrator say about the Queen?		
What things does the Queen say?		
In what way does the Queen speak?		
What sort of things does the Queen do?		

PHOTOCOPIABLE

A missing girl

- Use these notes and statements to help you write a newspaper report about Goldilocks' disappearance.

Upset Mother Bear said: "I don't know why she came in but she ate all the porridge and broke my favourite chair. I didn't actually see her." Angry Father Bear said: "She got into the bed with her shoes on and the sheets are filthy. I haven't seen her since." Poor little Baby Bear had a sore tummy and couldn't comment. Puzzled Mrs Nosy Parker said: "I saw Goldilocks sneak into the cottage. I didn't see her come out because I was busy."

Police statement:
Goldilocks was last seen entering the house of the three bears. She had left by the time the bears returned. Mother and Father Bear didn't see her leave. We are searching the woods. Anyone with information should contact police HQ.

Reporters use a mixture of direct quotes, like the statements above, and reported speech, like this:

Goldilocks' worried mum said her daughter had left the house after a hearty breakfast at 7.00am. She is begging Goldilocks to return home.

- Write some of your own quotes and then decide which you will include as quotes and which will be reported speech.

- Choose one of these concluding sentences or write your own:

It is now 24 hours since Goldilocks was last seen and local people are becoming extremely concerned for her safety.

Local police are saying that Father and Mother Bear are exemplary citizens and are not under suspicion.

Mr Wolf, mayor of Fairy Tale Town, has issued a statement asking for calm and reminding everyone that bad things don't happen in this town.

PHOTOCOPIABLE

Illustrations © 2010, Mike Phillips/Beehive Illustration.

SCHOLASTIC
www.scholastic.co.uk

Assessment

Assessment advice

Current educational research highlights the vital importance of structuring tasks that allow children time to develop as independent learners. Tightly focused tasks, with only one correct answer, create a culture of dependence. In order to assess learning, teachers need to observe and listen to children as they explore and discuss ideas.

Children need to take responsibility for their own learning by entering into partnerships with peers and teachers in the assessment process. Setting the criteria for learning tasks and knowing the criteria by which their work is being judged gives children control. Learners need to be able to evaluate quality. They will only come to know the standard and quality that is possible by sharing the work of others.

The following activity will allow you to observe and assess children individually and in groups. As they develop a presentation, the children are reminded that they are being observed and are informed of the success criteria. Feedback is given, along with the opportunity to improve *during* the assessment process. Children will sharpen their own learning through the analysis of others' progress.

Where more than one rhyme has been studied, groups should be organised according to their favourite rhyme. The activity should take place over four sessions.

Showcasing Revolting Rhymes

> **Assessment focus:** To respond imaginatively, using different strategies to engage with texts.
> **What you need:** Copies of *Revolting Rhymes*, copy of photocopiable page 32 for each child, access to computers, writing and art materials.

What to do

● Explain that it is the group's task to ignite interest across the school in Roald Dahl's book, *Revolting Rhymes*. They will be developing a showcase about one rhyme that will be assessed by the class, before being shared with other classes.

● In the first session, challenge the children to think of different ways they could approach the task. Ideas could include a short drama, an information poster, a recital of part of a rhyme or a PowerPoint or flipchart presentation. Explain that each group of five or six will prepare and then present their own showcase.

● Distribute copies of photocopiable page 32 and discuss Part B. This is a list of criteria by which the presentations will be judged by a peer group.

● Organise the children into groups and ask each one to decide on a name. Pair up groups and explain that these pairs will complete assessment sheets for one another, while the rest of the class observes. In session 2, ask the children to answer the questions from Part A of photocopiable page 32 individually. This is in preparation for the group task, but also for individual assessment.

● In session 3, tell the groups that their actual presentation must be no longer than ten minutes. Remind them of the criteria and allow one hour for preparation.

● Listen and observe, noting evidence of the knowledge that children have of the rhymes and of the language they use to negotiate with one another. You will also gain a great deal of information about their social skills, problem-solving skills and ability to collaborate.

● Talk to the children about the assessment you are carrying out as they work. Give feedback on this at the end of the session.

● In the final session, remind the children of your expectations. The groups will need another hour to finally polish their presentations. Then, encourage them to showcase their work, with peer assessment and feedback at the end. They can share their presentations with another class or in assembly.

Showcasing Revolting Rhymes

A. Use these questions to help evaluate your chosen rhyme.

Name of the rhyme: _____

What is the moral of the tale? Do you agree with this? Give reasons for your answer.

_____

_____

What is the funniest part and what makes it funny?

_____

_____

What is the most shocking part and what makes it shocking?

_____

_____

For what age group is this tale suitable/not suitable? Why?

_____

_____

Which character would you like to meet and what questions would you ask them?

_____

_____

B. Use these questions to help you discuss and evaluate another group's showcase presentation.

What type of presentation was it? What did you find most interesting? Which part did you find most enjoyable? Did every group member participate? How clear was the speech? How well was the group organised? What did you learn that was new? In what ways was the audience involved?